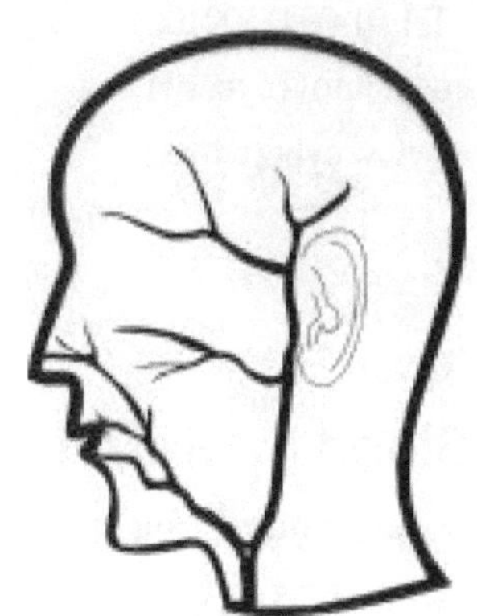

The Blood In My Veins

(Poems 1995 - 2005)

U.V. RAY

Cyberwit.net

HIG 45, KAUSHAMBI KUNJ,

KALINDIPURAM,

ALLAHABAD - 211011 (U.P.)

Tel: 91-09415091004

E-mail: info@cyberwit.net

www.cyberwit.net

The Blood In My Veins

(Poems 1995 – 2005)

U.V. RAY

Copyright© 2005 U.V. Ray

9788182530423

First Edition: 2005

Rs. 80/-

Typeset by Vaishnavi Enterprises, Kamla Nagar, Allahabad
Printed in India at Astha Associates, D. N. Marg, Allahabad

Dedicated to the young whore in Reno, who was the only thing that made my stay worthwhile.

ACKNOWLEDGEMENTS

I would like to thank the editors of the following magazines where some of these poems first appeared:

Smoke, Poetry Now, Iota, Voice & Verse, Dial 174, Page 84, Weyfarers, Candelabrum, Taj Mahal Review, Anchor Books, Poetry Monthly, Aesthetica, Slightly West, A Bard Hair Day.

Front cover image, U.V.RAY. Cover art & design by Mr. Kent Jensen (askejen@online.no)

ABOUT THE POET

U.V. Ray was born in Birmingham, England in 1967. He attended the Blue Coat School, but after dropping out of the "indoctrination system" at the age of 15 without any qualifications, he embarked on a life of hedonistic excess; spending the next 17 years of his life drifting around back street bars and nightclubs, surrounding himself with a colourful array of oddball characters and misfits. His life became a catalogue of bar room brawls, smashed up cars and trashed hotel rooms, with a little bit of writing in between. Most of his work during this tumultuous period was scribbled on beer mats and cigarette packets and has almost certainly been lost for all time. In 1993, U.V. Ray began taking his writing more seriously and he started submitting work to underground literature magazines. He had his first poem published in the Cambridgeshire magazine, Candelabrum, in 1995. The Blood In My Veins is a collection of some of his published works which were written over the subsequent decade. He lives and writes in Uttoxeter, Staffordshire.

CONTENTS

I Love You

Tonight
you immerse me,
just as the oceans immerse the earth.
Your eyes
are blue as the evening twilight
and your voice
carries your words
like a flower in the breeze;
you are beautiful,
amazing,
an almost uncontainable force –
and you intoxicate my very being
by just sitting here
amidst this hot summer flurry
of Cuban café discourse.

Late Night Death Song

A lingering kiss
sleeps only in the fire
and our slow love song
is nothing more
than a failing voice
echoing in the night.

White Swan

lies bleeding;
her red blood, stark
upon pure white feathers.
Broken winged
she gasps for air,
and with a final blink
of her great golden eyes
she slips away;
lost like a diamond
cast into a river.

To The Waitress In Café Brasilia

every now
and then
you catch me
with such
alluring
little glances;
those warm
olive-green eyes
intoxicate me,
over sweet cappuccino
in the morning.

For Paula

Love the way
you come in the palm of my hand

Like a writhing sea
caressing a shoreline of sand

Nothing At All

even a television set
has more soul
than most of the people I know;

yet this
is not the basis for emptiness,

but waiting
for a knock at the door,
a simple telephone call,
is.

the most inflexible chill
is needing someone

and finding only silence
as you reach for insanity
in some fragmented shrine
to nothing at all.

First Impression

dyed red hair,
long and unbrushed;
her faint smile
revealed
a slightly crooked tooth.

Big Shot

he
drives
a jet black jag,
wears
big
dark
glasses
and stinks of Chanel.
he
relishes
the
fact
that he agitates
and
plays
his
cards
at his absolute will.
but
he
lacks
any
real human spirit
and
his
life
is
just an empty shell.

The Resident Drunk

he stands
at the bar
all day,
drinking
neat whiskey
and puffing on
big fat cigars.
he reads
the obituaries
with
unnatural
enthusiasm,
boring the fuck
out of anyone
who'll listen
to his long
drawn out
stories
of lost
comrades
and far more
glorious days.

In My Heart I Know This

pretty girls,
just like
all the pretty flowers,
will one day
fade away
and die.

Transition

in her quieter moments
she might just think of you;
she will leaf through
the books that you gave her,
caress those silver ear rings
or recall the scent of your cologne.
she will remember you
with a brief moment of affection,
before slipping into stiletto shoes
and walking off to a world
where you do not belong.

Muse

your tongue
cool and moist
against my flesh

the perfect curve
of your soft
pink nippled breast

Opera

Sugar Sweet,
you still haunt
my sleep.

And like a stabbed prima ballerina,

the cut
is blood red deep.

Beautiful Girl

You are
elegant
expressive
vibrant;
just sitting in the coffee shop –
with your full red lips
and that chic haircut,
I wish you could begin to know
just how much
I like you so.

Woman

She washes husband's clothes
in the aluminium sink,
dark Gallic eyes
undilated;
she dares not speak or smile.

After Watching 'Le Mepris'

(A poem For Brigitte Bardot)

To think
that I could look upon
the wonder of a great blue sea
and yet this whole world
would mean nothing without you.

To never again
gaze upon your perfect body,
caress your porcelain skin
or trail my fingers through your hair.

To know
that you had once loved me
just as I had loved every part of you.

But how you tortured me,
how you tantalized and enticed me,
held me spellbound
with your infinite green eyes.

And to know that you are forever gone
is the pain of knowing
that missing you completely
is all that is left
that can be done.

Shining Star

You were born of beautiful soul
and I fear you will die too soon,

for this swirling ferocious world
could break your silken wings in two.

Somewhere In The Distant Night

Somewhere in the distant night a young woman sings
as the blue waves come crashing against the shore
and the sky glitters with a brilliance of pure white stars.

Between two worlds we lie stretched out on yellow sand
and amidst such breathless immensity of being
how could I not fall in love with your bright blue eyes?

Tender moments such as these can free a man's soul;
I seal your moist red lips with mine
whilst on the horizon, city lights sparkle green and gold.

The Poet In Question

With all the hullabaloo
that he could muster,
he very grandly announced
what he called
his formal resignation.
But when nobody noticed
his absence,
he very quietly
began writing
Again.

You Are A Flame In My Soul

Knowing you
is like
fresh birdsong
amidst
this swirling hurricane

She Flows Around Me

Naked, you are
pure as porcelain;
slender,
white,
translucent,
sad eyed, grey.
And you have a soul
that burns brighter
than carnival night
in Brazil.
You are exquisite,
your body, fluid
in movement
as a raging sea;
and I would drown
exhausted
in your love for me.

Pop Psychology

In this vast city
of eternal siren wail
and swarm;
I pick a leaf from a tree
and watch it gently
fall.

The Kimberly Hotel, New York

her

hot blood

rushes

through veins

swollen

with passion,

skin

flushed

as a pink rose;

while

beyond

hotel windows,

city lights

pulse

to the spark

of love's

momentary

fusion.

In BB's Café, Birmingham

8th September 2004

tea (cup) ————— £0.99p

served by Amy.

Waiting tables
like a distressed blonde actress –

an unforgettable
bright blue eyed princess

The Blood In My Veins

Sleep next to me,
young dark heart.
Let us sustain
this influx of silent desire,
let it flow around us
like a golden stream of fire;
breathe easy in my arms,
for you are as natural to me
as to the earth a flower.

Mentioning No Names

He is still
very much alive,
and writing
like there's no tomorrow.

He has been called
The Most Exciting Writer
In America!

Well God help
America.

Tired Of Society

I am drunk and spirit broken
naked on a hard granite floor
bathed in stark white light
of a bare light bulb

and when they find me like this

I will smile
that miracle death smile

for this world will flame on

but words like these
will simply
    slip
        away

The Painted Doll

she looked
like a faded
old actress
or something.
a little bit
sleazy
round the edges.
dyed blonde hair,
her cigarette
cocked high
in the air,
talked down
into her drink
as if nobody
was worth
the effort
of full blown
conversation.
the whole shebang
was like
an aloof scene
from
an art house movie
depicting
her own life story,
except
for the fact
that she had
nothing left
worth living for.

Between Us

one
hundred
rainy
days
have fallen
between
us.
my heart
spins
inside
me
like a
coin
on a
card
player's
table;
beating
louder
than
the
sum
of its
parts,
until
finally
it stops
and I
can

find
my
solace
in
the
bitter
sediment
at the
bottom
of
the
glass.

Desolation

She wears
a pink leather jacket,
used to be
a high class hooker
back in
the late seventies.
And although
she still looks good
her mind
has turned bitter,
she just slumps
against the bar
smoking Gitanes
whilst secretly hoping
they'll kill her.

Secret Letter To Poets

I see very little sincerity
in any of the poets I've met;
of course, they would vigorously refuse to accept
that writing is no more
than a slow form of show business,
or that they're too full of their own importance
to ever write a damn thing worthwhile.
But since even a charlatan
can occasionally stumble upon a fragment of truth
and inadvertently offer a hand of guidance
to the helpless, lost or potentially suicidal,
then it is of paramount importance
that we keep our big mouths shut
and say nothing of this deception
we seem to have established.

Presence

her beauty
has faded
now,
but the softness
in her eyes
is still
an undiminished glow,
and the simple
way
she paints her nails
can touch
your very soul.

Telephone

please don't call;
your crisp cotton words
reverberate
through my soul.

A Lost Moment

dark patches
beneath vivacious blue eyes,
a faint smile
upon a sensuous
lipstick smeared mouth,
soft blonde hair
twisted coyly around
her painted fingertips.
such indefinable beauty
etched into the face
of the girl
staring from a window
of the train
idling in
a Birmingham station.

Marilyn Monroe

I picture her there
upon a mattress, draped
like some delicate wraith;
a single unique raindrop
dissipated, lost
for all time
upon this dusky earth.

Hello, From New York City

I sit watching
the raindrops
evaporate
into the cracks
in the pavement
of New York City;
just waiting
for a glimpse
of the
Puerto Riccan maid,
who graces
my hotel room
as I drink my coffee
in the morning.

Waking Up With Sam

She whispers to me
beneath this grey morning sky;
her voice trembles
like a flower in the breeze,
and as jazz music plays
softly on the radio
she kisses me back to sleep.
Her skin is like milk
and it tastes apple sweet.

Girlfriend

even when
I try
to keep it
so simple
that it's
almost
childlike
it is still
so very
difficult
to find
the words
and explain
the reasons
why
I love you

Colours

because
politicians
are
spineless
and
afraid of foreign bloodlines
these
two
nations
will
collide

For Monica Bellucci

just one hour in your presence
could fuel a lifetime of desire

and the briefest touch of your lips
could crumble a man to dust

beautiful Italian actress
laughing all the way to the bank

Astronomy

You are like
a pre-renaissance painting,
where perspective
becomes lost in acquiescence
to the fluidic immensity
of your bright young being;
and we revolve as separate worlds
on different trajectories
endlessly spinning, alone
through time.

On A Chicago City Street

Stark
as a
black and white
photograph;
a girl who was
beautiful,
stood
so statuesque
amidst
the tempest
of siren wail
and taxi cab
horn blast.

9 788182 530423